PRAISES & ROSES

For who I was, am and will be.

JWEL

Dedicated to

All those who acknowledge the essence of life and poetry. (PS- Special spotlight to my family, friends and somehow sunshine.)

Introduction

"Medicine, law, business, engineering, these are noble pursuits and necessary to sustain life. But poetry, beauty, romance, love, these are what we stay alive for."

-Dead Poets Society (1989)

I've always wondered why I started writing poetry. At first, they were just poems, but over the years, they've evolved into something more, something I like to call poetries. I've always had a way with words and rhymes, creating a symphony with every line, every phrase, and every sentence in my mind. That's why I decided to pursue my passion in the world of literature and words. I love how playing with words and rearranging them can bring a sense of warmth and comfort.

Beyond the beauty of language, poetry has become a means for me to delve into new experiences and emotions, from tragedies and sorrows to passions and happiness. My work encompasses a mix of my own experiences, influences from literature, music, and various sources of inspiration.

Through my poetry, I strive to share unique emotions and perspectives, providing a glimpse into the profound depths of human nature and the complexities of life. While we may never fully comprehend everything, I believe in the importance of continuously expanding our understanding and connecting with others on a deeper level. I aim to delve into the intricacies of human nature, seeking to comprehend its nuances, for within its essence lies both light and dark, making for an extraordinary understanding.

I am not scared of the dark,
For it hides my wounds from the day.

Content

- APOLOGIES, CONFESSION AND TORMENT

STARDOM

I Yearn to go Home

Divine hung up in the dark.
My eyes capture it so very fondly,
Mesmerised by the audacity of this show so eloquently
teasing.
Pleasing.

I tried to get it, but it was all too far away-
Just giving me a glinting smile.
As if to try again.
Wish again.

Their vivid shine took my breath away
Their fame high. I admired them.
Awed

Aligning different stars, making beautiful patterns.

That's where I belong,
I am made of stardust-
My home is with them.
So vivid in the eclipse.

Starry Nights

These starry nights make me cry,
They shimmer and twinkle with the glow I have-
Yet I am dull.
A burnt front.
A crisp crust
Stardust.
I always devour these nights.
Hungrily.
Passionately.

Consuming it.
I count time with my eyes,
When I see the starry nights.

FAIRYTALE

Heavenly Havoc

The heavenly havoc of thy pulled me closer then,
Confuses me now.
Immature, you sure are.

Reckless,
Are all these emotions
Of the trust and need of mine.
Will let me down,
Will burn me up,
Will tear me apart.

Sunshine Glow

The wind speaks to me, and flowers-
They whisper.

When I see you,
You with your smile
Smile because of your smile!

Mesmerizing they are by the way you see,
the way you speak,
the way you shroud out every inch of vicious within me

Caramel eyes, you make me squirm.

When we look at each other
It makes me scream, beg and plead
For a world so warm and sweet
For a dream so utopian.
Bliss
Bliss
Bliss

I get lost in those brown eyes of yours.
When you look at me-
At the sunshine glow.

Clouds Remind Me of You

I look up to the sky and hear the breeze singing,
Hallelujah! It's Christmas!

The clouds, seemingly Persephone.
They dance with the wind,
Their moves soft and calm.

Mesmerised,
I stare
Thinking it's you
Taking me on this iridescent ride.
The throbbing beat of my heart.
As I look up to the sky-
The clouds.
They remind me who you are.

Somewhere
Somehow
I still have the strength to hold on to something
For someone,
someone to come and cradle me

Is that my sunshine?
My everglow?

-A distant observer

Life is a willow as it bends to your will.

-Person with the most beautiful eyes

Secret Conversations?

Purple hue at the top and you.
No hiss, no laughs-
A look passes between us.
Oh god, You're sun-
Son, you're fire.

Higher and higher heartbeats (mine) go-
To the heaven, I look and curse.
With a smile on my face,
And butterflies in my stomach.

Just envelope me already in your arms.
My home.
Like you've held me together with your words.
Your charm.

Sweetly, I come to you
Or rather-
Fly towards you.
My wings, your strength.
My smile, your smile.
A look passes between us,
Mesmerised.

Cherie, Let's Sing

Cherie,
Your eyes speak to me-
But today they sing!
They dance, they do-
Do everything to melt me.

I look away,
With mischief and young blush.
Your light touch on my face-
Electricity bolts within me,
And fireworks too.

Eye to eye, our hearts sync
Together they sing the same rhythm.
Same melody-
Same tune-
That you sing.

Loop of Eyes

I believe I have regressed many times
And each time I come back, it's to those eyes
War.
Peace.
Beauty.
A hidden melancholy in its melody
A hidden serpent in a wreath
A hidden wave in a calm sea
For something excites my being in this solemn existence
So I regress every night
And every idle stand by-
Just to know how it feels to live forever
Even if it is for a moment.

Frame of Love

Shimmering light in the sky-
Or are they in your eyes?
Mesmerised-
I stare at them hard.
Trying to decipher the language they speak.

A pity.
That you couldn't see the way I see you.
Pink hue.
In my thoughts, in my mind.

Frame of love
Of roses and lilies.

Trailing rail of calmness I feel when I see you
In my dreams.
In reality too-
You're a dream, and its true true true.
For now it's up to you.
To take it high
Leave it low
Shallow dives or drenching snow
For I shall forever stay in this frame.
The frame of love
Of roses and lilies.

Love is an Irony: I

This night brings turmoil in my life that seemed so
perfect-
The withering tentacles of illusion are grasping viciously
They're up and down and round and round
They choke you with strength so utterly profound.

For the ticking clock goes on-
And silence envelopes all
All I can hear is my harsh breath and hushed wounds.

Wanting to screech and cry out red on white
Which I presumed was twisting me foul
Like serpent. Insane.

In this dark void of confusion.
All I ask for is the hand I wish for
But the one I wanted has backed away
And left me tangled.
Alone.

Love is an Irony: II

All alone, I shiver.
As the hand caresses my running tears.
Soothing my painful years.
They try to push me-
In the tyranny of love.

Should I go? Should I stay?
"Does it even matter?" They say
Honestly, it doesn't anymore.

But it does, it does!
Everything does! Oh!
How small things affect us!

It's truly a miracle. Are we bound together?

Fate did play a joke on me,
Havoc in me, peace within you.

Alas, all I did was cry and cry
Cry and cry.
But why?
This tyranny of love
Might build upon me again.

But this time I won't bow-
I'll make it the prey.

Or I'll pray-

That everything turns out just fine.
The hand that withdrew comes to life.
To hold me.
To console me.

But who am I even kidding-
Fate plays jokes on me.
And these hands are pushing me in love.
What an irony.

DEMON-TALE

Mirrors on the Wall

Mirrors on the wall, time tickling by
Hushed cry of mine
And broken strands of promises.

I tossed them at bay.
Oh! To whom do I say?
To whom do I confide?
I feel cold on warm nights.

The holy bells ring but I can't even sing!
With all the sins I've committed: dark-twisted soul
within.

Mirrors on the wall show me my hollow life-
Holding broken strands,
Once called promises.

Dark Water

Oh, the dark waters!
Take me for a swim.
Take me to your place,
So I don't see the light again.

My tale will be told as a horror one.

I will subsidise under these calming waves.
Heaven will rejoice, and the angels will sing!
As I will and will struggle-
As I'll go with this water dark-
I'll go to my new home.

The sirens will sing a melodious tune,
Not a mourn will go around.
As I go for a swim in the dark waters
And the dark waters will keep me
For forever.

A Bit Too Harsh

Feel the cold whilst the sun shines bright.
Chills creeping up the spine.
I close my eyes and see their cry.
A disappointment yet a smile.
With tears in their eyes regretting what they did
And cursing the gods for having me.
Yet they shower me with love-
Which I am not worthy of.

Human's Art

We humans glorify pain.
And tragedy.
And sorrow.

That's why some of the finest arts bestowed,
Shoved
To the face of human existence are the bled wounds.

Bewitched by the sufferings of others and our own,
We make art.
And yet-
They're beautiful.

The mourning and mornings,
Are showering and blessings.
For we humans,
Transform anything into tragedy,
And tragedy to an art.

Where's My Mind?

What a total waste
Where's the calling that people talk about?
I feel so lifeless-
I have a home and a perfect body.
But where's my sound mind?
It is silent.
But a bit too silent!
No hums of interest,
No prayers of well-being.
Where's my mind now
Even when my body feels like a home.

This is My Agony

I have an agonising existence
That shred me to bones
And it is proved by the red scratches on my arms and
neck
That I impose to restrain myself from the greed,
residing in my heart.
I ache for someone who could read me
And tell me
It's not greed

It is not greed!

It's my torment
It's my suffocation
It's my agony.

Am I a Sadist?

I cannot deny of a sadist that I have become
I feed off the ills in my life
I do no deed to reminisce about them twice
However, they cannot remain alone
Hence, they took my core, a burning red ore
They ate it to strengthen themselves
Little by little, they tore my limbs
In my brain, they did the same in a stretch.
No, they're not inhumane
I cannot describe a part of me that way
For, you see, I too feed off them.

The Mourners

Mourn the mourners,
For they miss the spark of life.

Troubled by quests so strange-
Strangled by veins, so tight.
Weighted breaths they take,
Dreamless nights they pass.
Hollow skies they see-
And shapeless clouds that bypass.

Mourn the mourners
For they mourn to be mourned.
To feed their empty soul, they want to be mourned.

Petals of the last hawthorn fell,
But it was too late now.
Cherry season is long gone-
And no cherishing home.

Mourn the mourners-
The mourners are the mourn.
Seeds they sow, ripe winters fresh.
And it reigns on and on-
No end to the blizzard.
It is the mourn.

Maybe,
I am the problem.

What's the difference between life and existence?

If you ask me if I am alive, "Of course! You can see me breathing, eating, reading."
But am I really alive? I don't feel my heart pounding or any warmth on hot days. I don't see vivid colours-yellow, green, blue, red or smell the fragrance of daises. I haven't made a flower wreath for myself or anyone. Of course, I smile and laugh, but I am often called for the absence of shine in my eyes. I haven't jumped off the cliff holding my lover's hand under the moonlight and neither have I cooked for anyone as a token of appreciation. Am I really alive because right now my chest feels too still and my mind is too silent?
I haven't had blush because of enjoyment nor lost my breath because of the stunning scenery.

Am I really alive, or am I just existing?

Drinking Makes Me Sober

All struggle withering vines
Grapes of wine
Sour and high
I drink and drink till I am sober
Sober enough to handle this all over.

I am crushed and buried in Pompeii
My bones and ashes- my graveyard
An exhibition for people as they walk all over me
Whilst saying "Alas, what a tragedy!"

I am like a sunken ship
The Titanic bid me farewell as I sunk
Atleast it is mourned, I am not.
Opaque all around.

Withering vines of struggle
And wine grapes of agony
Together I drink and drink it over
I drink it till I am sober.

Memories: They Keep Me Apart

Silver lining midst the dark hue-
It's blue and grey.
Wreath of ol' memories
These moments create
Sweet aroma of old wine,
More time pass, higher the high
A basket full of sour and jelly beans
A land full of glooms and glees
That's what keeps me alive
That's what keeps me apart.

Rendezvous with a Bittersweet Memory

Sore toe in warm December
A warm hole in cold January
Page embraces my melted soul
These turned edges, a remembrance,
Of how I felt tracing the sides-
How I blushed when I thought of you and I
I wrote a song that I didn't sing
I built a home in which we didn't live
It was all for my memories-
For my sole mind
It was a haven,
A haven for my pride.
Sweeping my cherished pieces-
That were in the dark
Putting them in a deep slumber
For my sole heart.

"Sunshine all the time makes a desert."

- Arab proverb

All I have

Dead flowers between the pages of my book,
Phrases that are underlined.
The heart I drew, the scars that bled-
I hold it dear, Oh! Very dear
Because only that's what I don't fear.
The demised roses once pricked my vein
But in vain,
Oh! In vain
I still have the lines marked
The lines of scar
The lines of spark
Alas, now all that is left are these eyes.

Mirage
Everything midst the dust-
My sand castle didn't stand a chance.
And no ruins are left, no tears were shed
Time didn't stop-
And no one mourned.

"Because mourning is for the cowards, mourning is for
the weak."

I treasure my grains, my gains and pains.
But my hand is now empty.
And all I have is this book
With dead flowers buried in between.

Why Am I in Love with My Rage?

The rage could make me bear my life.
The rage would sweep me up and carry me.
Gently and lovingly
Enveloped in lush red and warmth
That makes the blood in my veins boil,
that makes my head pound.
Makes my cheeks flushed
And I perspire, uncoiling the resentment within me
Twirling the desperation within me
For my heart finally pounds
And I can hear it beat, beat, beat.
Rage is beauty, rage is morphine
For in it, I open up the closet of my deepest desires
Soak in the basking scorch of hell fire
Oh, how much I feel alive!

(How did I drown myself in the lucid frigid-
That I unknowingly fell in love with the burning
sensation
To finally soothe my cold fire within.)

-Rage makes me realise that I am alive.

My mind picks up on my heart
"You're so easy to play."
Heart plays a melancholy melody
"That's how you know I am there."

All in the name of pride
You drown yourself.

Moon Will Come for Me

Sincerely,
Moon faded into a translucent space.
But it took a part of me too,
It definitely did!
Why you ask?
I feel so lonely without it,
As if hung up in a consuming void.

Flashing lights of a masquerade ball
Held above my head fascinated me.
But my kins must have committed
Many, many, many sins,
Desisting me from making my debut
In the secular society of the sky.

Oh! But the moon visited me.
Praising me for my dress
And blush crept its face, keeping half of it hidden.

It visited me for nights and nights
And sometimes at dawn.

Our matching craters made us a pair!
"I'll come for you when the time's right."

And faded in the light
Grazing at me affectionately.

I always wanted to be in a fantasy world.
No wonder I became a target of love.

-Victim of Love

My Hidden Part

I am sure the part of me that can be loved is hidden
somewhere
And all I want is someone who can crawl there.
Through the small tunnels of my seclusion
With the eclipse that resides within me.
Soothe me of my desires and envies-
For I sometimes serve those masters
I let go of bounds that hold me together
I burn with passion so maddening that scarlet drips from
my lips.
And it scares me that I'll lose myself-
In the raging battle screams.

APOLOGIES, CONFESSIONS AND TORMENT

Praises & Roses

I sympathise with the one I was a few lives back
For someone who could not keep up with the regime
then
Like house of cards it was,
Built.
Rebuilt.
But I couldn't understand it that time
Couldn't cope with the speed of my approaching demise
Dwelled in the realms that shouldn't be lived in
Drank wine which shouldn't be drunk.

I sympathise with the one I was a few lives back
And hope for redemption in my present sense
For all the nine lives that I have lived
All I craved for was some praises and roses.

Let Me Be The Icarus

I resent Icarus.
He flew despite being called upon
A mere mortal tucked in thoughts of dreams did not haze
He flew despite being a flicker of life
He died enveloped in the embrace of Aqua
But he did not fade-
He did not fade!
Water at shore sang his tale
Icarus flew
Died.
But he touched the sky.

Whatever happens,
never lie to yourself.

In How Many Lives Did I Search For Myself

In how many lives have I searched for myself?
In the soft glow of burning kerosene
with frantic eyes and a yearning touch of self.

For grace and elegance in a delinquent is a feisty lie
How could a mob be a motif of virtue?
when they pursue crimson howls.

But I cannot say
And so I must refrain from saying so about myself
For I know it's all to keep the heart pounding
And to bring myself into existential meaning
To bring colours to my lifeless means.

I've searched for myself in lives before
And it looks like I have more to go
For I am like a breeze that sways on
and a thirst which rages on.

I often find myself in a hysteria of continuous drool and infatuation for a life away from my present identity.

All Over Again

I always knew you weren't right for me.
Yet I did-
Let you break it.
This isn't fair!
But I let you do it.

I let you hold it, and gave you the key
Of all possessions that humans possess protectively.
Let you play with my feelings, let you break it into
pieces-
So they cannot be joined again.
I always knew you were my destruction.

When I looked into your eyes
I knew I wouldn't have the courage to back away.
I knew you were the Lucifer,
Here on the Earth to seduce me again.
Yet I gave in.

When I knew the end was with me broken again,
With my mute mouth and shouting pain.
I ain't your property I used to say.
But we both knew how much I was in vain.

All the lies, all the cries were always mine-
But whenever I saw you smile on my stained face-
I knew I was the pawn whom you used to play

I don't remember how bright was the Sun,
Or how vivid were the colours of the outside world.
Staying in your shadows has devastated me.
But I swear to god if you come again,
I'll have to go with these emotions all over again.

I am too young for such heavy emotions.
My heart and body might be unable to withstand the
depth of consolidation my soul yearns for.

Flashback: The Dark Alley

Pieces of the world that you were to me,
Pierce my skin as I walk upon millions of them.
Trying to move on, trying to get a grip
Of what I did-

Beside a silent building, a road so full of pain
It wasn't raining. It was you and I
Then I did something that made us apart.
I took your hands and pushed you afar-
I witnessed your beautiful face crumbling.
Into something so unknown-
I never knew I was capable of something so sore.

But you got it, you let me go
My timid act-
Of course, shook you to core.
But aware of my bidding.
You let me go.
You let me free.
You let me be me.

I cannot thank you enough.
And I fully accept the blame-
I fully invite those ruthless eyes and pointing fingers.
As if saying "She's vain."

Finally, I left you in the dark alley
Pouring rain-
Down your face were the streaming tears,
Aching of your broken heart-
Echoed in the dark shadows.

I see you're much better than before
But the dark alley still haunts me.
I would never forgive myself
And the coldness that holds me.
You told someone-
"Maybe she has moved on. But she won't love him like
me."

It will take time.
It will take time.
Maybe I too will forgive myself
Because whatever I did, it was for me.

-Anna Karenina holds me dearly.

Thank you guys for reading this book. I hope you find it really really thought provoking (and interesting for that matter). It might look good in your instagram feed or pinterest page for all that it matters. Kindly support it if you find it good and I'll very much appreciate it.

To catch on the thoughts and some deep discussions or maybe adding on some of your views or just maybe correcting me in some of my observation and judgement, feel free to mail me at praises.roses@gmail.com.

Have a good day!